CRACKING
THE
INHERITANCE CODE

The Missing Link for
Transferring Wealth Without Drama

CRACKING
THE
INHERITANCE CODE

The Missing Link for
Transferring Wealth Without Drama

Cindy Arledge

Praise for Cindy Arledge and
CRACKING the Inheritance Code

"After forty years as a financial planner I see people spend more time planning their vacation than putting their financial affairs in order. Cindy's experience and her simple direct approach makes it crystal clear and easy to take action. The big WHY leads directly into the WHAT and HOW."

—James Stewart, Certified Financial Planner, retired and National Social Security Advisor, retired

"Cindy Arledge has walked through the fire of family wealth devastation and lived to write about it. Now, out of this painful experience comes her latest book, *CRACKING the Inheritance Code*. In it, Cindy shares with us her many gifts for creating transformational solutions to help others avoid a similar fate. *CRACKING the Inheritance Code* is a must-read for any family looking to maintain two of the most important things in life, family wealth – and even more importantly, family harmony."

—Douglas D Box, Family Business Consultant

"One of the most meaningful outcomes for our lives is to leave a legacy for generations to come. In *Cracking the Inheritance Code*, Cindy Arledge offers powerful tools to leave a financial legacy that will allow your family to thrive after you're gone. In doing so, she also offers another gift: her philosophy for leveraging this process to forge stronger family bonds and 'make the rest of your life the best of your life.' This unique combination of the financial, the emotional and the spiritual make this book a must for anyone who wants to have an impact on this world."

—Pam Hendrickson, best-selling author, Product and Content Creation Expert

"Cindy's message is needed by so many people. Her powerful story will help families address this topic before the family leader passes away. This book is a must have for anyone who values strong family relationships and positively impacting future generations."

—Chris Stark, Knights of Columbus, General Agent

Praise for Cindy Arledge and
THE LEGACY FAMILY WAY

"Cindy has written an important book on the power of money to both build and destroy families. Her insights into money and values are especially helpful as families work together to navigate the difficult path of legacy, both with their resource of money, but also with the values they wish to pass down to generations. Cindy gives a blueprint for how to speak with family members about money and inheritance, before the death event occurs to help preserve family relationships. This book is the guide to having those difficult conversations now instead of at an emotionally charged, tense meeting in a lawyer's office. Use this book to plan ahead to save hurt feelings, misunderstandings and preserve family legacies."

—Anne-Marie Faiola, CEO and Founder, Bramble Berry ® Inc.,
and author of *Live Your Best Day Ever*

"Grief after death is expected, but the additional drama created by unprepared heirs is optional. Legacy Family Planning is the tool smart families use to protect their family's future."

—Dean Lindsay, author of *The Progress Challenge,*
Big Phat Goals

"I wish that this book was available before my situation with my family crashed. Hopefully it will not be too late for you. This book is crammed full of good advice and easy to read."

—Dennis De Naut, World Traveler,
Photographer of Light

"Cindy is both inspirational and cathartic. A general Wow! Now, I know where to go and what to do. Although it will evolve over time, I have a good starting point."

—Don Rector, Vice President, TPO Business Development,
Caliber Home Loans

Praise for
CUR$E OF INHERITANCE

"I speak from experience when I counsel you to read and take to heart what you learn from this book. Ignorance is not bliss when it comes to inheritance. Adopting this information will not only change your life, it will improve the entire dynamic of your family."

—Bobbi Schwartz, Founder and CEO of
Be Iconic Style

"My husband and I have been real estate investors for more than 20 years. We are all too familiar with the Cur$e of Inheritance. We've seen countless homes over the years owned by heirs of unplanned estates that end up in foreclosure or taken by the county for property taxes. The family ends up with broken relationships and no proceeds from what is often the most valuable portion of their loved one's estate. Over and over again they say, 'I never expected this from my siblings.'"

—Toni D'Angelo-Lott, HomeVestors,
We Buy Ugly Houses™ Franchisee

"It isn't often we get simple advice for complex problems, but Cindy Arledge has managed to succinctly navigate the complexities of inheritance. Whether you are the beneficiary of an inheritance or the benefactor, this is a must read for the entire family. She writes from the heart and mind, and is straight forward and full of empirical data."

—Kathy Miner, Award-winning 5-Star Realtor

"A masterpiece that clearly defines wealth transfer conversations that families must have NOW to protect future relationships."

—Lauren Midgley, Time Behaviorist and
author of *It's 6 a.m. and I'm Already Behind*

Praise for
My Camino, My Life

"Cindy's humorous and inspiring story is a great read for anyone considering walking the Camino or seeking more out of life."

—John P. Strelecky, #1 best-selling author of
The Why Cafe

"Cindy Arledge is a spirited and heart-centered entrepreneur. Her journey across the Camino is an inspiration. I admire her ability to turn grief into power. She can help you live with purpose, prosperity and joy."

—Mastin Kipp, best-selling author of
Daily Love: Growing into Grace

"I didn't know I needed the lessons, but they leapt from the pages and into my soul! I found myself smiling throughout the tale, and I could imagine myself right there with her. Cindy's insight and thoughts spoke to my heart and purpose."

—Brenna Smith, Founder and CEO
SheNOW, LLC

"Cindy takes you on a journey that will make you laugh, cry and think about your own path. Grab several copies and pass them out to all of the people you care about."

—Kate Delaney, Business Motivational Speaker
& NBC Talk Show Host

CRACKING the Inheritance Code
The Missing Link for Transferring Wealth Without Drama

Copyright © 2018 by Cindy Arledge
Published by: Legacy Inheritance Partners, Ltd
All Rights Reserved

5100 Eldorado Parkway, Suite 102-703
McKinney, TX 75070

Cover design by Brian Moreland
Interior layout design by Brian Moreland
Illustrations by Lisa Rothstein
Graphic design by Maggie Hicks

ISBN 978-0-9826953-6-4

Disclaimer

This book is sold with the understanding that the publisher and author are not engaged in rendering legal, accounting or other professional services. Anyone planning to take action in any of the areas mentioned in this book should seek legal and expert assistance of trusted and competent professionals.

With the exception of the author's personal experiences, any similarity to actual people or places is coincidental. Names and places have been altered to protect confidentiality, and many stories are a compilation of actual experiences known to the author. Examples of Avoiders, Acceptors and Anticipators are the author's opinion only and are based on known facts concerning status of will and behavior of family members after death.

Every effort has been made to make this book as complete and accurate as possible. However, there may be mistakes both typographical and in content. Therefore, this text should be used only as a general guide.

The purpose of this book is to educate, empower, and inspire action. The author and Legacy Inheritance Partners, Ltd shall have neither liability nor responsibility to any person or entity with respect to any loss or damage caused or alleged to be caused directly or indirectly by the information contained in this book.

Upon receipt of purchase, if you do not wish to be bound by the above, you may return this book to the publisher for a full refund.

Acknowledgments

To the Creator, thank you for transforming my mess into a message to help others.

To Brittany, I celebrate and love you. Thank you for the honor of being your mom.

To Gerald, my dear husband, thank you for supporting my desire, nay, need, to be closer to the grandchildren and picking up the pieces that I drop. You are my rock.

To Christian, Emory, Aizlynn, and Avery, thank you for inspiring me to be the best I can be and teaching me how to love unconditionally.

To our unborn generations, you were loved before you arrived.

To you, dear reader,

May you find inspiration and practical advice

to define your legacy, live your best life,

and use your gifts and talents

to make the world a better place.

Table of Contents

Introduction

According to Benjamin Franklin, "Nothing is certain except death and taxes." While taxes may be certain, they are avoidable with a good tax plan. Death, on the other hand is unavoidable. Logically, we would spend more time and energy planning for something we cannot avoid. But death is an emotional topic, and one we hesitate to accept, or face.

Our avoidance of the unavoidable creates unnecessary drama for our families, and us. When we "suddenly" find ourselves in the midst of chaos, be it medical emergency, temporary need of help, or facing an end-of-life situation, our lack of planning adds to the confusion.

What happens when you anticipate the inevitability of death instead of trying to avoid it?

What if you approached planning for your death with the same determination you approached tax planning?

What if planning for the uncomfortable and unavoidable was the secret to a life of meaning and purpose?

What if CRACKING the Inheritance Code to transfer wealth without drama was the roadmap for fostering lasting family relationships? I'm talking about relationships that stand the test of time, generation after generation.

What if the answer was *irony*? That living life with the end in mind was the secret for making the rest of your life, the best of your life? That facing challenges, and preparing your family to face challenges was the tool to help them thrive in your absence.

Irony is defined as an event that seems deliberately contrary to what is expected. Irony is the silver lining, the ability to transform challenges into opportunities. Embracing irony helped me turn the biggest mess of my life into a message to help you.

As you read this book, be alert for examples of irony. My goal is that by the time you finish, you will have joined me in my practice of embracing irony as a way of life.

There isn't a day that goes by that I don't smile with appreciation for the lessons I've learned through irony. Rejection taught me to accept myself. Hate taught me to love. Death taught me how to live my best life.

The tagline of this book, *The Missing Link for Transferring Wealth Without Drama*, suggests that the benefit of this book is for your family after you are gone.

Truth is, *you* will benefit the most from this read. This book is for you. The ideas, tools, and steps will help you expand your vision of the future, meet challenges in a new way, and enjoy life more. The side benefit is a drama free wealth transfer for your heirs.

You will discover the peace and confidence that comes from defining your legacy and facing death. You will learn how preparing to die becomes the roadmap for living with significance, and how preparing your family to thrive in your absence brings you closer together.

You will learn how expanding your vision to live with the end in mind is the key to making every minute count.

How will you accomplish this so quickly? This book is divided into three sections after this introduction:

In Part One: A Fresh Approach, you will have a new approach to an age-old problem. After reading this section you will have a thorough understanding of why wealth transfers fail and be introduced to an assessment to measure your current level of preparedness.

In Part Two: What You Don't Know That You Don't Know, you will discover new definitions for legacy and wealth, a process that can protect your family's future, take the assessment introduced in Part One, learn what it means for you and your family, and debunk one of the most common myths about owning your own business. After reading this section, you will have the information and tools to define your legacy and your life's impact, as well as determining your current level of preparedness.

In Part Three: Three Steps for CRACKING the Inheritance Code, you will discover three simple steps you can take to transfer wealth without drama. After reading this section you will have the information and tools to complete the steps and protect your family's future by embracing the irony of defining your legacy and facing your mortality.

Why I Wrote This Book

This is my third book on Legacy Family Planning. It fits in between my first legacy book, *Cur$e of Inheritance*, and my second book, *The Legacy Family Way*. While both books deliver innovative information, after they were published, I realized there was a gap between the two. I needed to provide a launching pad: "start here" and "what's in it for you and your family."

This book provides you with that starting point, a place to decide if Legacy Family Planning is right for you, and your family. It is a place for you to discover what you don't know that you need to know. It is the place to discover the missing link for transferring wealth without drama.

In *Cur$e of Inheritance*, I tell my story and introduce readers to the problem, the solution, and the monster.

The Cur$e of Inheritance is an ugly monster of jealousy, fear, and selfishness that crushes families, eats money, and destroys lives.

The Cur$e of Inheritance is born in an environment of loss and grief, by unprepared heirs who feel entitled to unearned wealth, and tragically forget to see each other as human beings.

The Legacy Family Way provides Do-It-Yourself (DIY) instructions for implementing the Legacy Family Planning process. It is an excellent next step after you finish this book.

If you can, read *Cur$e of Inheritance* first. You will understand the "why" behind my passion for Legacy Family Planning and desire to help you. If not, don't worry, this book gives you all the information you need to get started.

The following definition powerfully sums up the real issue behind most inheritance failures.

Inheritance failure is defined as a loss of assets, destroyed relationships, and unnecessary upheaval. Inheritance failure means the financial capital you worked so hard to earn doesn't benefit your family. Your children and grandchildren lose touch, or worse, end up in ligitagtion, and their grief is compounded by the turmoil of broken relationships.

I wrote this book to give you the information you need to protect your family so that they won't have to go through what my family endured. My aim was to provide you with the information you don't know that you don't know. My desire is to inspire you to add the missing link for transferring wealth without drama so that your family doesn't end up being broke, bitter, and blaming you.

Why You Should Read This Book

If you've ever felt the pain of a lost relationship, or witnessed someone else's pain after the loss of a loved one, you are familiar with the long-term devastation caused by inheritance failure. Sadly, up to 90% of relationships are negatively affected after a death in the family.

You will gain valuable insight on how and why this phenomenon occurs. More importantly, you will learn how to beat the odds so that you can protect your loved ones.

If you are concerned about how your heirs will respond to their inheritance, you will benefit from reading this book. It contains the antidote to affluenza, spendthrift behavior, and entitlement. When you complete the suggested steps, you will be more confident about the impact of your legacy.

If you want to expand your wealth but feel frustrated with your financial position, I have exciting news. Your financial assets are but a piece of the puzzle. You will discover additional forms of wealth to enrich your legacy.

If you are passionate about positively impacting the world, you will be delighted to discover the expanded definition of legacy, and tips for making the rest of your life, the best of your life. When you define your legacy, you create a roadmap for living with the end in mind. A life you love to live, and a legacy you love to give.

This book isn't for everyone. Not everyone has the desire to leave financial assets to heirs. Not everyone has a desire to positively impact the world. As harsh as it sounds, not everyone wants to live their best life. If you are closed-minded, or don't have the desire to positively impact your family or community, this probably isn't the book for you.

However, if you can identify with any of the following categories, this easy-to-read book will introduce you to a fresh approach to a difficult topic and three simple steps you can take to protect your heirs from unnecessary drama after you are gone. You might even discover a career you never knew existed.

- You are a member of a blended family.
- You have children and/or grandchildren.
- You own a family controlled business.
- You want to positively impact the world.
- You expect to receive an inheritance from a parent, grandparent, or loved one.
- You love to be informed and learn new information.
- You have a friend or family member who fits into one of these categories.
- You advise clients to grow or manage their finances, provide legal, tax, or other estate planning services.
- You are longing for a business with a purpose to help others, or you wish to expand your existing business.

This book is more about you, and how you'll spend the rest of your life, than it is about what you will leave behind. This book will change the way you think about legacy, estate planning, and the advantage of preparing to die so that you can love living your legacy.

Why Now?

We are in a historic moment in time. Just search the Internet for *greatest wealth transfer history mankind* and discover a plethora of articles on this topic.

According to *InvestmentNews*, conservatively, over 30 trillion dollars of wealth will transfer in the next 30 years. Baby boomers are setting the stage for this epic event, not only with the money they saved, but with inherited gains from their parents. The number of millionaires is increasing through business opportunities and wealth transfers.

If you are expecting to be on the receiving end of this transfer, on the surface, it probably sounds pretty awesome. You have a windfall headed your way. Except for the loss of your loved one, that is.

If you are like me, a baby boomer, or the oldest living generation in your family, you may be proud of your contribution to history. My estate planning goal is to bless my family. Give them an opportunity to thrive in my absence. And to be remembered. Fondly.

But what if there is a hidden dark side to this greatest wealth transfer in the history of mankind? Darker than the death that precipitated the event.

What if this historical event was the catalyst for destroying 90% of the families it touched? Instead of families benefiting from their inheritance, it destroyed lives, relationships, and bank accounts. What if this greatest of wealth transfers was harmful to the people it was expected to help?

Cumulatively, what if this historical transfer of wealth became the catalyst for destroying our nation?

The family is the smallest economic unit of society. Destroy the economic integrity of the family, and you can destroy the economic integrity of a nation.

Through the eyes of someone who has lived through a failed inheritance, our nation is facing a tragedy of epic proportions that most people have yet to recognize.

The American family is clueless to the greatest threat it has ever faced: The Cur$e.

If this sounds farfetched, or the ramblings of a lunatic, please stay with me and allow me to explain.

There is a proven process that families use to successfully transfer wealth from one generation to the next. Most likely, you just haven't heard about the secret estate planning tool that, until now, has been reserved for ultra-high-net-worth (UHNW) families. If you don't have at least 35 million dollars, you don't qualify for support from the "family office" industry, which means you haven't had access to this process. This is tragic, because it doesn't take much money to destroy a family. I know, because it happened to my family.

Before I share my story, I want to be crystal clear: I am asking you to join the Legacy Family movement by inspiring you to add legacy family planning to your estate plan, and/or join the growing team of trained legacy family planning advisors.

My mission is to bring affordable Legacy Family Planning to dedicated family leaders who don't have access to the information they need to protect their family's future.

The danger is real.

Now is the time to increase awareness and access to the solution to prevent the tragedy before it happens.

My goal is to inspire enough families to stop the impending financial crisis. My goal is to inspire you.

> *"You either have to be part of the solution, or you're going to be part of the problem."*
>
> ## — Eldridge Cleaver

My Story

In 2015 I walked 500 miles across Spain to complete the Camino de Santiago, an ancient pilgrimage in Europe. My purpose in completing the walk was to test a *formula for living* that I had developed to heal from the emotional devastation that followed my parents' deaths.

I call my formula GRIPP Life™. GRIPP is an acronym for Gratefully, Responsibly, Intentionally Pursuing Purpose. Although I had developed plantar fasciitis before the trip, I intended to prove the power of the GRIPP Life™ Formula by completing the walk with Ease and Grace.

When I returned home, I wrote my first book, *My Camino, My Life: A Sole to Soul Connection*. In the writing process, I became a witness to my own healing and discovered, instead of sharing the GRIPP Life™ Formula, it was time to start a revolution to help others avoid the needless pain and suffering I endured from our family's failed inheritance.

Becoming an orphan is painful, at any age. It didn't matter that I was 46 when my parents passed away eight months apart. I felt lost and alone. The feeling was compounded by the unexpected loss of emotional support from my three older brothers. The people who had known me my whole life, the ones I had counted on to help me navigate life without our parents, had disappeared. Instead of supporting each other in our grief, we were consumed with business decisions, sibling rivalry, and legal battles.

The "dark night of the soul" is an ancient term to describe an inner state of lost hope. A disconnection between life's purpose and meaning. A time when you hit your knees in prayer, but don't feel that your prayers are heard.

I was consumed by three questions. What did I do to deserve so much pain? What do I need to do to stop the pain? What am I supposed to learn?

Discovering the answers saved me. They led me out of the darkness. Like others who have come before, I have turned my mess into my message and discovered my life's purpose. I share my story to inspire you to avoid the pain I suffered.

The challenges my brothers and I faced after our parents' deaths are not new, and we are not alone.

A few years after my parents passed away, I was appalled to discover our family was just another sad statistic of the "shirtsleeves to shirtsleeves" three-generational cycle of wealth loss.

Sadly, my parents did everything they knew to do to prevent our tragedy. They hired professional advisors to craft an elaborate estate plan to reduce our tax burden, and legal documents to distribute their assets. They used the estate planning tools and best practices that were available to them at the time. The preparation they took was necessary and appropriate. It just wasn't enough to prevent the breakdown of their kids' relationships, large legal fees, confusion, and uncertainty.

They followed ALMOST all the advice they received. The parts they didn't follow created a huge tax liability that Dad forewarned me about. I remember thinking, "It's his money and if he wants to spend it on taxes, he can."

Dad was aware he had created a challenge, but he didn't know how to prepare me to co-sign the $1,833,385.12 IRS check.

He cautioned me about potential relationship issues. But I was wearing rose-colored glasses and refused to believe his predictions.

What Dad didn't know would have kept his hard-earned assets in the family and prevented the legal action between his children.

Dad spent a lifetime training me to take his place in the business. Too bad, he didn't know how to unite our whole family as a team to protect and grow the assets under our care.

Rest assured, I don't blame my dad. Looking back, I can see he anticipated many of the problems that unfolded after his death. He did his best to prepare me with the information he had at the time.

But, it wasn't enough. Make no mistake, *what he didn't know* resulted in lost assets, destroyed relationships, and unnecessary pain and suffering for his children and grandchildren.

Ironically, it's what my parents didn't know that could have saved us. Although financially successful, they didn't have 35 million dollars. Had they been able to reach this level of wealth, they could have hired advisors from the "family office" industry and discovered the secret to transferring wealth without the drama. ***They could have discovered what they didn't know: Legacy Family Planning.***

I believe that if my parents had known about Legacy Family Planning, they could have prevented the heartache we suffered, and kept their hard-earned wealth in the family. Legacy Family Planning is what you need to know to protect your family.

By the time you finish this book, you will have the foundation you need to begin adding Legacy Family Planning to your estate plan. You will have:

- Identified your legacy
- Discovered the three aspects of legacy
- Recognized the five types of capital

After you finish this book, and complete the three simple steps, you will be ready to begin adding the missing link to your estate plan.

Before you begin the process of Cracking the Inheritance Code, I want to share a poem that guided me out of the dark night of the soul. I hope it provides you a path to follow and helps you as much as it did me.

In the Crypts of Westminster Abbey, an Epitaph from the Tomb of an Anglican Bishop (AD 1100):

When I was young and free and my imagination had no limits, I dreamed of changing the world. As I grew older and wiser, I discovered the world would not change, so I shortened my sights somewhat and decided to change only my country.

But it, too, seemed immovable.

As I grew into my twilight years, in one last desperate attempt, I settled for changing only my family, those closest to me, but alas, they would have none of it.

And now, as I lie on my deathbed, I suddenly realize: If I had only changed myself first, then by example I would have changed my family.

From their inspiration and encouragement, I would then have been able to better my country and who knows, I may have changed the world.

How to Get the Most from This Book

Like *Cur$e of Inheritance* and *The Legacy Family Way*, this book is easy to read. But it contains a lot of new information.

I hope you write in the margins, underline or highlight ideas, and use the notes at the back of the book to capture action items and notate the ideas you plan to follow up on.

I've written this book for baby boomers who have children and/or grandchildren. If you aren't a baby boomer, or family leader, please know you will still benefit from learning the information I've put together.

Part One

A Fresh Approach

No One Is Getting Out
of Here Alive

Everyone Over 18 Years Old Needs a Will

Just in case you missed the disclaimer, I'm repeating myself here, because it is important that you know: this book does not provide legal advice. Please, contact your professional advisors for legal advice.

For the purposes of this book, "will" is the group of essential legal documents you need to protect yourself in case you become incapacitated or die.

Please note: your will protects you while you are alive and protects your family after you are gone.

If you don't have a will, you are not alone. According to a 2014 *Forbes* article, 51% of Americans between the ages of 55 and 64 don't have a will. Men are more likely to have a will than women. When considering younger age groups, the number of people without a will dramatically increases to 64% who lack protection.

If you become incapacitated, what decisions do you want made on your behalf? Who will make them for you? Without a will, it doesn't matter what you want, you haven't legally appointed anyone to act on your behalf.

And if you are the parent of underage children, you and your children are especially vulnerable. If you don't have a will, you have placed your children's future in the hands of your state government.

The conversations you've had with your children's god parents, your relatives, or friends don't matter. Without a will, no one has any legal rights. Even if you have godparents designated, your state will decide their guardianship. Don't risk their future because you haven't taken the necessary steps to protect them.

You wouldn't let your children play with a loaded gun. You wouldn't let your children play on the freeway. Avoid putting their lives at risk because you don't have a will.

If you are a parent of adult children, please help them complete this important first step. Did you know, that unless your young adult has a medical power of attorney in place, you don't have the right to receive medical information in case of emergency?

If this describes you, do not pass go, do not collect $200, contact a professional advisor and get a will. I've heard all the reasons why you don't have one yet. They don't matter. If you're over the age of 18, you need a will. End of story. Contact a professional and get the protection you need.

Action Item: Make an appointment with a professional to obtain your will. If you don't know who to call, ask your mom, dad, best friend, or other professional advisor. You can do this!

Most people think money is the problem.

They are wrong.

AVOIDING DEATH IS THE PROBLEM!

Death makes us uncomfortable. We act as though we aren't going to die.

We do our best to avoid thinking about it, talking about it, or preparing for it.

And for those who have a will, the vast majority remain uncomfortable with the idea of dying and do the minimum to prepare.

In other words . . . even when we legally prepare for death, we aren't comfortable facing our mortality.

Isn't it interesting that we resist, avoid and ignore the **one thing** that life guarantees?

MONEY IS AN AMPLIFIER

Money is amoral.

It is neither good nor bad.

It only makes you more of who you are.

More money **amplifies your current relationship with it.**

If you're generous, more money makes you more generous.

If you're greedy, more money makes you greedier.

If you're confused, like I was, more money makes you more confused.

Inheritances fail because heirs haven't been prepared.

COMPLICATING THIS PROBLEM...
unearned wealth is cursed.

Things received without effort come
with a spiritual attachment.
You may know it as "a free lunch."

The Kabbalists call it
"the Bread of Shame."

The Bread of Shame
is a little known, but powerful force.

Just ask any lottery winner!

Inheritance is an insidious form of the Bread of Shame. Think about it for a moment. Someone had to die first.

(Presumably, a loved one.)

Without preparation, unearned wealth received after a loved one's death feels dirty.

This is called:
The **Cur$e** of Inheritance.

Up to 90% of
of wealth transfers fail.

By fail, I mean

breakdown of the family unit,

loss of financial assets, and

emotional upheaval for family members.

Family members are left uncertain,

confused, and unprepared.

Entire family lines can split apart.

Relationships are lost forever.

Isn't it time to fix
this broken system?

Why have we accepted this broken system as normal?

Death and money are taboo topics.

We don't understand the real issue.

We lack access to a viable solution.

We don't know what we don't know!

3 Generational Cycle

Generation 1 creates wealth.

Generation 2 receives inheritance.

By the end of the third generation,

the wealth is gone.

The odds of heirs retaining their wealth are historically low. Worldwide, throughout history, 75- 90% of wealth transfers fail within three generations. This is called "shirtsleeves to shirtsleeves" in the United States, "clogs to clogs" in Ireland, and "rice paddies to rice paddies" in Japan.

Why is there so much drama?

Why do family members fight over inheritances?

The Importance of Perspective

Words have meaning. During my research I was curious about the dictionary's definition of legacy and inheritance. What I learned shocked me and opened the door to a new level of awareness for inheritance failures.

Legacy is what you leave behind. *Inheritance* is what you receive. In other words, legacy is seen through the eyes of the giver and inheritance is seen through the eyes of the receiver.

There is a big difference between these two perspectives. My dad was proud of the legacy he worked so hard to create. He came from a broken family and grew up poor during the Depression. According to my aunts, many of the homes they rented didn't have running water or electricity.

His childhood experiences fueled his desire to become financially successful. From his perspective, the games he missed and the time spent away were the sacrifices he made to achieve his dreams. Achieving financial security is an admirable goal, but when is enough *enough*?

Through a child's eyes, there is no correlation between the empty seat in the stands at their sporting event and the food you put on the table. The child doesn't see that you're not at the game because you're hard at work earning money to support the family and build wealth for the future.

As adults, we can make the connection, and appreciate the sacrifices made on our behalf. Children, on the other hand, are often hurt when their parents aren't around for the important events. Those childhood hurts can be resurrected during the grief process, after you're gone.

The time to share your perspective will have passed. Without understanding why you made the choices you made, your heirs can get stuck in an emotional well of darkness.

Siblings can experience very different relationships with their parents. An older sibling, held to strict compliance with the rules, may wonder at the freedom that the baby of the family enjoys.

In addition to the perspective difference between givers and receivers, there can be vast perspective differences between heirs. Adult children can get stuck seeing each other from childhood points of view. The labels we give each other stick. Instead of recognizing each other's adult accomplishments, education, and skills, the "bed-wetter," the "smart one," and the "troublemaker" are the heirs who settle their parents' estate.

My brothers saw me as the "widdle sister" despite earning my master's degree in business, obtaining my Texas real estate broker license, and receiving years of on-the-job training from Dad.

Communication and trust issues can also be caused by distance, lack of interaction, differences in values, lifestyles, and beliefs.

When these clashing perspectives, lingering childhood stories, and lack of communication and trust collide during the already trying time of loss and grief, it's easy to understand the source of the emotions that are ready to be unleashed during the wealth transfer process.

When givers fail to see how their gift will be seen through the eyes of their heirs, the givers can unwittingly unleash the Cur$e of Inheritance.

What's in store for your family?

Once you understand the real problem isn't money, you can create a real solution! Yes, money is part of the problem, but the real issue is our avoidance of death and failure to prepare our family. It is easier to prevent the Cur$e of Inheritance than it is to recover from it. Believe me, I know.

"An once of prevention is worth a pound of cure."
— Benjamin Franklin

It's been almost twelve years since my parents passed away. Until last year, I co-owned a piece of property with a brother who still refuses to speak to me. Now we are no longer business partners.

I had hoped we could repair our relationship after we ended the business. I left him a message on his cell phone to share some interesting family history that I knew he would enjoy. Sadly, he texted my daughter to inform her that he had deleted my message without listening to it and to tell me "to never contact him again."

Despite my inability to heal this relationship, I am very grateful to him. He has taught me a valuable life lesson. I have the capacity to love someone who hates me. I'm not angry with my brother, just sad. Sad that he is missing out on love. From me and my family. Based on his recent response, he will probably never meet his great nephew and nieces.

If you haven't prepared your legacy, then after you're gone, the Cur$e of Inheritance is near impossible to cure. It is much more effective to prevent the Cur$e than it is to tame it.

But, there are exceptions. Surviving the Cur$e can bring family members closer together. Although my other brother, Richard, and I were not close growing up, we have become quite close in the past few years.

Richard was falsely convicted of money laundering and sentenced to 16 years in prison. If we hadn't been through the Cur$e toghether, it would not have occurred to me to extend my role of matriarch to him and his family.

The Cur$e of Inheritance is preventabale by becoming aware of the danger, and your level of risk, so that you can take action. To help my clients determine their risk and identify the steps they need to take to protect their family, I created an assessment to help my clients determine their current level of preparation.

The Legacy Pyramid is designed to help you quickly find your location on the pyramid and determine your family's expected outcome. The better prepared you are for death, the better the expected outcome for your family.

The Legacy Pyramid consists of two sides with three levels each. The left side of the pyramid **shows your personal level of death preparation.** The three levels are *Avoider*, *Acceptor*, and *Anticipator*.

The Legacy Pyramid

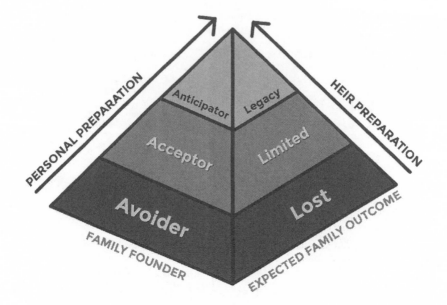

The right side of the pyramid **predicts your family's future based on your preparation**. What you do matters and directly affects your family's future. The three levels are ***Lost***, ***Limited***, and ***Legacy***.

My dad used to say, "If you don't know where you are, and don't know where you're going, how will you know when you arrive?" Later, in Part Two, you will have an opportunty to complete the assessment. In this section, I am introducing common sense concepts that few people think about.

Avoiders leave Lost Families
Acceptors leave Limited Families
Anticipators leave Legacy Families

Before We Move On, Let's Recap

No one is getting out of here alive.

Everyone over the age of 18 needs a will.

The real issue is our avoidance of death.

Money is an Amplifier.

The Cur$e of Inheritance is real.

The Three Generational Cycle of Wealth is a world-wide issue.

Unresolved differences of perspective cause unnecessary drama.

Introduction to the Legacy Pyramid Assessment.

Part Two

What You Don't Know

That You Don't Know

What You Don't Know

My friend, Will Morris, says, "you only die once, you better get it right." There are no second chances when it comes to estate planning.

In this section you will discover what you don't know that you don't know. Use this information to transform your attitude towards death; use it to become an Anticipator. Use this information to create your Legacy Family. In this section you will learn:

- The three aspects of legacy

- The five capital accounts

- The legacy family secret

- The missing link for successful wealth transfer

- Take the Legacy Pyramid Assessment to determine your location

- What to expect for Avoiders, Acceptors, and Anticipators

- The family business myth

Become an Anticipator
to Avoid Family Drama

Your action, or inaction,

will impact YOU

and your family

for generations to come.

Three Aspects of Legacy

Have you ever noticed that when you think about something you start seeing it everywhere? When I was looking for a new car to buy, I became interested in the Lincoln MKX. Once I identified it as the car I wanted, I started seeing them everywhere. It seemed like everywhere I looked, there was another MKX!

As a Legacy Family Planner, I think about legacy a lot, so it makes sense I notice it everywhere, especially in advertising. Advertisers recognize that baby boomers have entered the stage of life that significance matters. What better way to get our attention than to use legacy in an ad!

Harley Davidson wants me to know that "I can live my legacy and live life on my own terms" if I ride one of their motorcycles.

After the Galaxy Note 7 was banned from airplanes, Samsung launched an advertising campaign with a slogan "Innovation is our *Legacy*. Quality is our Priority."

Merriam-Webster's Dictionary has three definitions for legacy that include:

1. a gift by will especially of money or other personal property: Bequest;

2. something transmitted by or received from an ancestor or predecessor or from the past;

3. a candidate for membership in an organization (such as a school or fraternal order) who is given special status because of a familial relationship to a member.

How about you? How do you define legacy? In the space below or on a separate sheet of paper, put pen to paper and write your definition of legacy. Please don't read any further until you complete the exercise, so that you have a personal point of reference moving forward.

_____

_____

_____

_____

_____

_____

_____

I was frustrated after researching the definition of legacy. I couldn't find any definitions that provided guidance on creating my legacy. I couldn't find any instructions on how to transfer my legacy to my heirs. Since I couldn't find a definition that suited me, I made up my own.

My definition of legacy has three aspects. It includes *possessions*, what you leave behind, *memories*, how you want to be remembered, and *experiences*, how you want to experience life.

My definition has become a guiding force in my life. By turning the aspects into questions to be answered on a daily basis, I enjoy living the life I want to live and give.

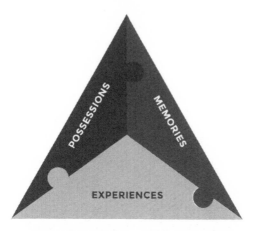

Asking the right questions is key to creating a life of significance. To define your legacy, ask and answer the following three questions every morning:

- What do I want to leave behind?

- How do I want to be remembered?

- How do I want to experience life?

At the end of the day, check in with yourself. Did you live your legacy today? What legacy moments did you create? What could you do better tomorrow? Your life is a journey and you determine the course. This end-of-day reflection is a powerful tool for living in alignment with your legacy. Be consistent and be amazed.

In Part Three, I will provide some tools to help you harness the power of these questions. I use these tools to face life challenges with courage, humor, and Grace. When you use them, they will help you, too. Live each day as a gift.

The Five Capital Accounts

Wealth is more than financial assets. Like legacy, wealth is another one of those words that has different meanings to different people. And, over time, our own definition of wealth can change.

While I agree that health and happiness are forms of wealth, for the purposes of *this book*, wealth includes the following five capital accounts: financial, intellectual, social, human, and spiritual.

In my previous books, I excluded spiritual capital from the definition, because I wasn't ready to tackle such a personal topic. Committing ideas to print takes courage. It isn't easy exposing my most vulnerable parts.

Over time, I've discovered the ideas that are the most difficult to share have the greatest impact, so I've pulled up my big-girl panties and included spiritual capital in this book.

Defining my own legacy, and assisting clients with their legacies, has taught me that defining legacy without including spiritual capital is like building a house in the sand. Spirituality is the cornerstone of the human experience. For many, spiritual capital is their most valuable asset, and is central to their Legacy Family Plan.

Spirituality has different meanings to different people, so don't worry that I'm going to try to tell you how to experience your Spirituality. I've just experienced and observed that our spiritual beliefs, whatever they are, are the heart center of Legacy Family Planning.

In preparation for defining your legacy in Part Three, as you read each capital account, think about who you want to impact with each one. To help you, please answer the question at the end of each account.

Let's start with **financial capital**. In its most simple form, you can measure your financial capital by measuring your net worth. The greater your net worth, the more choices you have in life. You've probably heard it said, *money can't buy happiness*, but it can solve a lot of problems. Your financial capital is the resource that provides choices in life to solve, and prevent problems.

Who do you want to impact with your financial capital?

____   Yourself

____   Your current heirs

____   Unborn generations

Intellectual capital includes innate learning styles and the collective knowledge you possess. Knowing your natural learning style and creating a lifelong learning goal increases your intellectual capital.

If you are a business owner, it also includes your expertise. My dad was an expert in locating real estate for car rental companies. Because he didn't know how to transfer his intellectual capital, our family lost his super power. Currently, we are re-inventing our real estate management company and capturing the intellectual capital we are creating to prepare future generations.

Who do you want to impact with your intellectual capital?

____ Yourself

____ Your current heirs

____ Unborn generations

Social capital is defined as the amount of "collective good" you provide with the time, talent, and treasure you donate in service to others. Measuring "collective good" gives you a tool to make informed decisions on the highest and best use of your valuable resources. Measuring and comparing are the keys to obtaining the highest impact for your donation, whether it is time, talent, or treasure. Giving to others increases gratitude, which is the antidote to entitlement.

My daughter, Tiffany, and I recently attended a seminar on impact investing. We are both intrigued by this value-based investing model and the resources available to identify companies that align with our values. Knowing that we can invest our financial resources to increase our wealth while improving the world is very exciting.

Who do you want to impact with your social capital?

____ Yourself

____ Your current heirs

____ Unborn generations

Human capital is you and your family, both current and future generations. Investing in the accumulation of health, emotional intelligence, skills, personality, intellectual capital, motivation, conflict resolution, communication, and self-development increases their value to themselves, and the family. It's about becoming the best version of yourself.

Investing in our family's Human Capital has already paid rich dividends. As a family, we have completed several assessments that have improved our ability to communicate and accept each other.

Who do you want to impact with your human capital?

____   Yourself

____   Your current heirs

____   Unborn generations

Spiritual capital includes, but is not limited to, your beliefs about religion, God, or however you refer to your Higher Power, how you respond to events beyond your control, your creative powers, the meaning behind life events, how you see yourself and others, the meaning of life, forgiveness, acceptance, death, what happens after death, heaven, hell, and . . . Spiritual capital is the ability to understand life, your purpose for living, and Faith.

Who do you want to impact with your spiritual capital?

____   Yourself

____   Your current heirs

____   Unborn generations

The Legacy Family Secret

When you want to find a solution to a problem, don't study failures, study success stories. During my research to protect my family, I discovered Legacy Families and the secret estate planning tool they use to successfully transfer wealth from one generation the next.

It's time to expand this solution to families like mine and yours, so that we can change the trajectory of inheritance failure created by the greatest wealth transfer of all time. From my own experience, I know you don't have to be ultra wealthy to beneift from using this tool.

We are in the middle of a financial crisis that has been ignored for far too long. **Legacy Family Planning is the missing link for transferring wealth without drama!** It is the key for preparing your family to receive their inheritnace. It is my goal to bring Legacy Family Planning to the masses so that we can protect families at risk. Add this estate planning tool to your current plan to prevent the Cur$e of Inheritance.

When I discovered what I didn't know, it made so much sense that I couldn't understand why I didn't see it before.

"All truth passes through three stages.
First, it is ridiculed. Second, it is violently opposed.
Third, it is accepted as being self-evident."

Arthur Schopenhauer's words of wisdom inspired me to share the missing link. My goal is for you to see Legacy Family Planning as self-evident in time to save your family.

The Missing Link

How can you prepare for something you don't know? In a study done by the Williams Group, 3,250 families surveyed over twenty years helped identify the two most common reasons for wealth transfer failure. This survey provided the critical information to design a real solution to prevent inheritance failure. Respondents reported that 1.) unprepared heirs and 2.) lack of communication and trust were the two biggest contributors for failed inheritances.

It's just common sense that prepared heirs who trust each other and can communicate have a better chance of successfully transferring wealth without drama. But common sense wasn't enough to devise the solution. Twenty years of scientific study became the basis of a new industry, one where legacy family planning experts are now being trained to prevent estate planning failures.

Legacy Family Planning doesn't replace any of your existing plans, or professional advisors. You still need your attorney to create your legal documents. You still need your CPA to assist with tax planning. And, you still need your wealth advisor to grow and protect your wealth. A Legacy Family Planner is an advisor who can help you create a sustainable family-first culture to prepare your heirs to receive their inheritance and carry your legacy forward.

Don't wait for a diagnosis or crisis. Now is the best time to add a Legacy Family Planner to your team.

Where are you on the Legacy Pyramid?

In the previous section you were introduced to the Legacy Pyramid.

Now, it's time to take the assessment, discover your location, and determine your family's expected outcome.

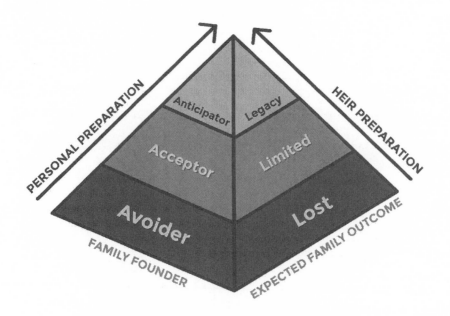

This is not a pass or fail test.

LEGACY PYRAMID ASSESSMENT

This 10 question assessment won't take long to complete. Don't overthink the questions and trust your first response. Choose the answer that best fits your current situation.

1. My heirs' response to their inheritance is:

A. ____ not my problem
B. ____ my advisors' responsibility after I'm gone
C. ____ my responsibility

2. When I think about discussing death, I am:

A. ____ uncomfortable, I won't do it
B. ____ uncomfortable, but I will do it
C ____ very comfortable

3. My estate plan:

A. ____ is on my "to do" list
B. ____ includes a traditional plan
C. ____ includes traditional & Legacy Family Plan

4. Has my family reviewed my Estate Plan?

A. ____ No
B. ____ They know I have one, but haven't seen it

C. ____ Yes, the entire family has reviewed it

5. Control of my assets:

A. ____ belongs to me
B. ____ will transfer after I'm gone
C. ____ is established by our governance plan

6. At the end of my life, my financial plan is:

A. ____ to bounce my last check
B. ____ will be revealed by my will
C. ____ is already known by all family members

7. My focus is upon:

A. ____ today
B. ____ my current heirs, children and grandchildren
C. ____ unborn generations living 100 years
from now

8. After my death, my financial resources:

A. ____ won't matter, I'll be gone
B. ____ will be used to take care of my last needs,
my family can fight over what's left
C. ____ will bless my family and/or community

9. The social impact of my finances is:

A. ____ not important
B. ____ important
C. ____ defined in a Stewardship Plan

10. In our family:

A. ____ most everyone gets along
B. ____ we try to get together for special occasions
C. ____ we meet regularly for family meetings and fun

Record Your Totals Here

Count the number of times you answered
each letter and record below.

Total of A Answers _____

Total of B Answers _____

Total of C Answers _____

Total of all Responses _____

Should total 10

Calculate Your Score

Transfer your totals, complete the multiplication for each level, and add together to determine your score.

Total A Answers _____ X 1 = _____

Total B Answers _____ X 2 = _____

Total C Answers _____ X 3 = _____

Total points: = _____

WHERE ARE YOU
AND WHAT DOES IT MEAN?

If your answer to question 3 is "a", it doesn't matter
what your score is. You are at the Avoider Level
and your family is a Lost Family.

If you scored between 10 and 19,
you are at the **Avoider Level**
and your family is a Lost Family.

If you scored between 20 and 25,
you are at the **Acceptor Level**
and your family is a Limited Family.

If you scored between 26 and 30,
you are at the **Anticipator Level**
and your family is a Legacy Family.

Download additional assessments at:
www.legacyfamilyrevolution.com/assessment

Avoiders and
the Lost Family

If you don't have a valid will, your first step
is to execute one.

Your Lost Family's future will be
determined by your state's law.

Without a valid will,
both you and your family are
in grave danger.
(pun intended)

Your action, or inaction, will affect your family for generations to come. Please, for the sake of your family, take this first step and get a valid will.

If you continue to be an Avoider, what can you and your family expect?

The outlook is grim.

Because you are unprepared, your family will suffer unnecessary heartache. Don't shoot the messenger here, but it's the hard truth. Not only have you placed your family in danger, you are in danger as well.

The Danger for you:

Without your Power of Attorney for Health Care, and DNR, should you become incapacitated, family members don't have the legal ability to make decisions on your behalf. If you become terminally incapacitated, doctors are required to make heroic efforts to keep your body alive for as long as they can. It doesn't matter what you want, how painful it is, how much it costs, or how long it takes.

The Danger for your family:

Your state laws will decide who receives your assets.

If you have underage children, your state laws will determine their guardianship.

The cost to settle your estate will increase, leaving less assets to care for your family.

**You don't think the government is going to take care of
your business for free, do you?**

If you received this book from an advisor, please contact them.
If obtaining a will is not their expertise, they will refer you to
someone who can help.

If you are an Avoider with a valid will you are to be congratulated!
While you have taken the most important first step in protecting
your family, you have a ways to go.

Remember, this is a journey.

It doesn't matter where you start.

It only matters where you end.

I know this is not an easy topic to explore. I implore you to have
the courage to keep reading. Avoid giving up on yourself or your
family. If you find yourself getting angry, good! Anger is a compass,
pointing you in the right direction.

The purpose of this part of the book is to enlighten you to the
reality your family faces and TAKE NECESSARY ACTIONS TO
PROTECT YOUR LOVED ONES. I'm not sugar coating anything. It's
time someone told the truth. If you haven't taken this critical step,
hopefully you will take heed, and take action.

YOU ARE NOT ALONE.

The following people died without a will.

They were *Avoiders*.

Prince
Sonny Bono
John Denver
Howard Hughes
President Abraham Lincoln
Rita Hayworth
Martin Luther King Jr.
Tupac Shakur

**Without a will,
you remain an Avoider.
Avoiders leave Lost families.**

Acceptors and
the Limited Family

If you have a valid will, but haven't prepared your family, your next step is to complete the three steps in this book, then create

a Legacy Family Plan.

Your Limited Family has the legal capacity to settle your affairs, but do they have

the proper training?

Without a Legacy Family Plan,
your family is subject to inheritance failure.

Your action, or inaction, will affect your family for generations to come. Please, for the sake of your family, add a Legacy Family Plan to your estate plan.

As an Acceptor, what can you and your family expect?

The outlook for the Limited Family is better than lost families, but remains a gamble. By preparing your will, you have provided your family with the legal tools they need to settle your estate. But failure to prepare your heirs means they are still subject to communication and trust issues that can destroy your family and waste precious resources.

The Danger for you:

Acceptors aren't comfortable talking about death. If you haven't clearly communicated your end-of-life desires with your **entire family at one time**, you are laying the foundation for misunderstanding and arguments that can happen after your death. Reliance on paperwork without communication with your doctor increases the likelihood your medical wishes for your final care will not be honored.

Later on, you'll hear Dan's story and see how being an Acceptor isn't enough to protect you, or prepare your family.

The Danger for your family:

Your legal documents are a solid foundation for your family's protection. But they aren't enough to protect them from the Cur$e of Inheritance—drama and infighting that can tear a family apart. The majority of wealth transfer failures happen due to a) communication issues and b) the gap in estate planning created by unprepared heirs who lack the ability to trust one another. Funds that could have gone to loved ones end up in the pockets of attorneys. It is not the attorney's fault, either. They provide services that consumers demand. Lawsuits are the effect of broken relationships. Heal the cause, broken relationships that create lawsuits in the future.

Limited families often suffer unnecessary pain and agony that are avoidable.

Most Acceptors have done all they know to do. It's what they don't know that they don't know that destroys the family.

The good news is, after reading this book, you will know the secret for transferring your wealth without the drama and prepare your family to help you when you need it.

Most likely you already have a team of professionals to help you prepare your estate plan. Most likely, your team includes a CPA, wealth advisor, and attorney. Most likely, your team has never heard of Legacy Family Planning.

Unless your advisors support UHNW individuals or particpate in the family office industry, they don't know what they don't know either. It's not their fault. Legacy Family Planning is the best kept secret hiding in plain sight.

Inheritance failures aren't caused by legal documents. They are caused by unprepared heirs who don't trust each other and can't communicate.

Legacy Family Planing is the missing process you can add to protect your family. Legacy Family Planning is the secret to protecting your family from being broke, bitter, and blaming you.

Legacy Family Planning is your family's protection from the Cur$e of Inheritance. The Cur$e is an ugly monster of jealousy, fear, and selfishness that crushes families, eats money, and destroys lives. There are no winners when the Cur$e is unleashed. Everyone is a victim.

If you received this book from an advisor, please contact them. Most likely, they work with a Legacy Family Planner who can help you create your plan.

Remember, this is a journey.

It doesn't matter where you start.

It only matters where you end.

YOU ARE NOT ALONE.

The following famous

and not so famous people

were *Acceptors*:

E. K. "Sandy" and Janice Arledge
(the author's parents)
Reginald and Gloria Morgan Vanderbilt
(Gloria Vanderbilt's parents)
Michael Jackson
Andy Warhol
Leona Helmsley
Aristotle Onassis

It's not the amount of money that unleashes the Cur$e. **Money amplifies** broken relationships that existed before the wealth transfer.

Staggering to consider, legal preparation isn't enough to protect your family.

Anticipators and the Legacy Family

You are an Anticipator if you have demonstrated the courage to prepare for your death so that your family can thrive in your absence.

You have seen your legacy through their eyes and prepared them to receive their inheritance.

You have created a Legacy Family Plan with your family.

You are confident about your family's future.

Your legacy will bless
future generations to come.

What can you and your family expect?

The outlook for the Legacy Family is optimistic. Your family has a plan to follow to carry your legacy forward. You have provided them with the training, skills, and direction to flourish in your absence.

The Benefit for you:

You have spent considerable time and energy to prepare your family. It hasn't always been easy, but it has been rewarding to see them grow. You invested in their success and enjoyed seeing their progress. They didn't have to wait for you to die to receive their inheritance. You were there to share it with them.

One of the greatest benefits of becoming an Anticipator is your ability to *own your life*. Every minute becomes precious; each day is a gift. Your life is your legacy, and as an Anticipator, your calendar and checkbook shift to match your values. You live significantly by daily reviewing the answers to the three aspects of legacy.

The Benefit for them:

Your heirs are confident in their ability to honor your wishes. They don't have to guess what you want because they helped you define your legacy. They have a plan to follow and the skills, talents, and desire to receive your legacy.

YOU ARE NOT ALONE.

You are a part of a very elite group.

The following families

and family-owned companies

are *Anticipators*:

Kongo Gumi, Japan, 40th generation,
construction, founded in 578

Barovier & Toso, Italy, 20th generation,
glass making, founded in 1295

Zildjian Cymbal Co., United States, 14th generation,
cymbals, founded in 1623

Nordstrom, United States, retailer, 4th generation,
founded in 1901

Cindy Arledge and Gerald Fritz
(the author and her husband)

Become an Anticipator.

It is the roadmap for making
the rest of your life, the best of your life.

When you become an Anticipator,
you know the joy and satisfaction of
creating a Legacy Family!

Remember, this is a journey.
It doesn't matter where you start.
It only matters where you end.

The Family Business Myth

There are many myths about owning a family business. But the myth I'm talking about, the one my parents believed and I bought into, is this: the family business is the best vehicle for transferring wealth to subsequent generations.

Although I enjoyed working with my parents for decades, when I married Gerald in 1997, I left their company to start my own family business with my new husband.

Several years later, we sold our franchise to spend more time with our teenage girls. I went to work at Countrywide Home Loans while Gerald managed our real estate portfolio. As a commissioned loan officer, I could earn unlimited income, and had access to quality health insurance.

When Dad was diagnosed with lung cancer in November 2004, my position with Countrywide had changed. I was now part of a small team who was responsible for recruiting, boarding, and training loan officers throughout the entire country.

Twelve months later, both my parents were gone. During that difficult year, I juggled my full-time job, served as co-executrix, had major surgery, and managed the day-to-day operations of my parents' real estate investment company.

It was too much, something had to give. That something was my career, and my health insurance. I took a temporary leave of absence to sort things out, then realized I couldn't serve two masters. With great sadness, I left my career to fulfill my obligation to my parents.

Had I known it would take years to obtain a clearance letter from the Internal Revenue Service (IRS), I might have made a different choice. But, I didn't know what I didn't know.

By the time we received the IRS letter in the summer of 2007, I was at my wits' end. Through mediation, we legally settled our disputes, but for months, my siblings and I didn't meet without the presence of our attorneys. I was devastated, and ready to move on with my life.

But there was a major hiccup in my parents' estate plan. Mother was an Alzheimer's victim and couldn't change her 1997 will. Dad made several changes in the ensuing decades which resulted in an incompatibility in the grandchildren's portion of their estate.

When we received the IRS letter, it was time to distribute the assets. The stumbling block was the grandchildren's portion of the estate. The most efficient and practical method to resolve the issue was to sell the assets in their limited partnership. The majority of which was four pieces of commercial real estate.

For a variety of reasons, all my brothers passed on purchasing the properties. Rather than wait to sell them to outside investors, I set aside my personal value of fiscal conservatism and jumped on the opportunity.

First and foremost, I wanted to honor my parents' desire for my children to receive monthly rental income. Buying my nieces' and nephews' shares in the partnership meant my children could retain their ownership in the real estate.

Second, it was the fastest way to settle the estate and earn my freedom. From the time Dad was diagnosed in November 2004 to the middle of November 2007, I suffered emotional abuse from several family members. I always knew I could walk away from my obligation as co-executrix, but made the choice to stay to end.

It wasn't easy to remain, but putting up with the abuse was a sacrifice I was willing to make for my parents, and my children. By November 2007, I was anxious to be free.

Last, but not least, I wasn't paying attention to the economic climate and was naive about the possible impact on our future. Gerald and I borrowed several million dollars to purchase the real estate at 100% of a 2006 valuation. We set aside our aversion to debt and grew our $100,000 house mortgage to several million dollars. This was a few months before the 2008 financial crisis. OUCH!

After we settled the estate, for the first time, I was free to run my business my way. Although Dad had spent considerable time and effort to teach me the business, I quickly discovered that his way wasn't my way.

It took several agonizing years to separate actual business knowledge from his strong personality style that I had interpreted as business knowledge. It was an emotional roller coaster. Of course, it didn't help that I was juggling crushing debt in a downwardly cycling economy while trying to figure it out.

I didn't even realize my belief about transferring the business was a myth until I discovered a delightful novel, *Every Family Business* by Thomas William Dean, Ph.D. After reading his book, I discovered what I didn't know about transferring family businesses.

Here're the facts. Fewer than one third of businesses will survive the first transfer. Less than 12% will make it past the second transfer, and only 3% are intact for the fourth generation to manage.

Some of this attrition is part of the normal business cycle. In his article, "Family Business Survival: Understanding the Statistics," Dr. Craig E. Aronoff makes an excellent point. Only one business, General Electric, survived the first 100 years of the New York Dow Jones Industrial Average. Any business, family owned or not, has a very slim chance of surviving four generations, or 100 years.

There are several factors that complicate transferring a family business. How will working and non-working family members work together?

My favorite pizza is but a distant memory because two brothers inherited equal halves of the business after their mom passed away. The non-working brother demanded "his half of the profit" without setting foot in the restaurant. Meanwhile, his brother was putting in 70-hour weeks. Rather than fighting a losing battle, the brothers closed the business forever, leaving raving fans of their 54-year-old establishment longing for one more bite of childhood comfort food.

What if your business is in a disrupted industry? Or, your product becomes obsolete? When was the last time you bought film for a camera, or ribbon for a typewriter? When you travel, do you call a cab, or use an app to select an alternative ride? Do you stay in hotels, or rent an entire house?

Making decisions becomes more complex with each successive transfer. The sole proprietor is a dictator, able to make decisions without consulting anyone. The second generation is typically a partnership. By the third generation, and beyond, decisions become more complex, requiring a cousin consortium.

Including the family business in your estate plan may NOT be the best plan. Perhaps, it's better to sell the business at the height of its value, either to passionate family members who are willing to risk their own funds, or to third parties.

Selling your business *while you are alive* is an opportunity to reduce drama after you are gone. Talk to your children and/or grandchildren. What are their interests and capabilities for buying the business from you?

Until I discovered what I didn't know, I was on the same path of perpetuating the family business myth with my children. But, now that we have new information, we are making different choices. We have a new plan unfolding that you will read about in later chapters.

Do you own a family business? Please consider how this will affect family relationships. Look 100 years into the future and plan accordingly.

Before We Move On, Let's Recap

The three aspects to legacy include your memories, experiences, and possessions. Each morning and evening, review the answers to the three important questions.

The five capital accounts include financial, intellectual, social, human, and spiritual.

We discovered the secret of successful wealth transfer.

Legacy Family Planning is the missing link for successfully transferring wealth and cracking the inheritance code.

You completed the Legacy Pyramid Assessment.

Discovered what you and your family can expect at the Avoider, Acceptor, and Anticipator levels of the Legacy Pyramid.

You debunked the family business myth that the family business is the best vehicle for transferring wealth to subsequent generations.

Part Three

Three Steps for

CRACKING the Inheritance Code

Three Simple Steps

The secret to transferring wealth without drama is as simple as one, two, three.

1. Live your legacy.

2. Prepare yourself.

3. Prepare your family.

Before we get started on the solution, let's take a moment to consider two concepts about the term *simple*.

We will begin with Albert Einstein's quote:

> *"When the solution is simple,*
> *God is answering."*

I believe Legacy Family Planning is God's answer to the current broken system of wealth transfer. Legacy Family Planning is the missing plan that gets to the heart of the issue.

Let me explain. Life is a gift from God. What we do with our life is our gift to God.

Legacy Family Planning is the most effective tool you can use to define your legacy. When you begin and end each day by answering the three aspects of legacy and act in alignment with your values, you define your gift to God. Defining your legacy (your gift to God) puts your life purpose at the heart of your estate planning efforts.

Traditional estate plans are the mechanisms to transfer your assets to your heirs, but are not designed to help prepare your heirs to receive their inheritance.

Legacy Family Planning is different. It not only provides you with a tool for defining your legacy for the five capital accounts, it serves as a playbook for the rest of your life, and a tool for preparing your heirs while you are here to help them.

The first step for transferring your legacy without drama is to *live your legacy*. With intention, you create meaningful memories and experiences, and prepare your family to steward what you leave behind.

This simple tool is God's answer to help you honor the gift of life you have been given, and provide a sustainable system for teaching future generations.

The second concept to consider about the term simple is this: Simple doesn't mean easy.

In fact, simple can be quite hard. Take weight loss for example. Losing weight is simple. Just consume less calories than you use, and it's easy to lose weight. Simple yes, easy no.

Eating is more than calorie consumption. Our ability to control our calories is affected by many factors that include stress, bad habits, addiction, taste, texture, allergies, fear, and hormone imbalance, just to name a few.

Transferring wealth without drama is the same. The process is simple, just three steps. But simple doesn't mean easy. There will be times the process is very easy. Other times, the process may be hard.

Don't be afraid of the difficult times. When you take a moment to reflect on your proudest accomplishment, my sense is, it wasn't easy. Perhaps you spent years earning your degree, learned a new skill, or overcame a tough challenge. My point is, overcoming difficulty can be very rewarding. What could be more rewarding than defining your legacy and preparing your heirs to receive their inheritance?

Now that we have explored the term *simple*, let's take a broad look at the three steps.

The first step, *live your legacy*, is a lifestyle choice of living with the end in mind. Your focus for this step concentrates on the three aspects of legacy. How do you want to be remembered? What do you want to experience? What do you want to leave behind? Answering these questions allows you to experience a significant life that matters to you.

To move from avoiding or accepting death to anticipating death is huge. With over 50% of the population lacking an estate plan, it is evident that this first step has been a stumbling block to many people. Don't let this be you.

The focus for the first step is to draw your line in the sand. It is the ball that starts everything rolling. Pick any metaphor you want, just do it. This step begins with deciding to act, then spending the rest of your life living your legacy. Fact is, all the steps are lifelong processes.

The focus for the second step, *prepare yourself*, is tidying up your life and putting your affairs in order. Simply put, you prepare to die. Ironically, doing so is the key to spending the rest of your life grateful for another day.

The focus for the third step, *prepare your family*, is preparing your heirs for success after you are gone. For the best results, invite your family to join you in the process, and get help from a professional.

In the following chapters you will discover information that you won't be able to forget. Ideally you will embrace what you learn and decide to embrace the legacy lifestyle and implement the missing link for your family.

Or, you won't decide to act. Either way, you will know what you don't know. You can always change your mind later. Hopefully when you do, it won't be too late for you and your family.

The process for CRACKING the Inheritance Code is simple: Live your legacy, prepare yourself, and prepare your family.

From my experience, this process is a divine gift that helps me show up as my best self. I am living my legacy, creating memories and experiences, so that I will be remembered the way I want to be remembered. It is the tool I am using to prepare my children to receive their inheritance. I know the pain of the Cur$e of Inheritance, and I don't want that for my family.

This simple process is not always easy. But what great accomplishment has ever been achieved without effort? I can't think of a greater accomplishment than living my legacy.

Step One:
Live Your Legacy

When you live your legacy, you create an internal compass that helps you show up as your best self in all situations. Only you know the answer to the three aspects of legacy questions:

- How do I want to be remembered?

- What do I want to experience?

- What do I want to leave behind?

Living your legacy is a lifestyle of responding to life's challenges in a manner that is satisfying to you. It's a lifestyle of creating moments to treasure. It's easy to be your best self when life is going your way. But what about when life doesn't go your way?

Keep your answers to the three aspects of legacy next to your heart.

- Behave in the manner of how you want to be remembered.

- Create experiences with intention.

- Determine what you want to leave behind.

Life is very satisfying when you live your legacy. You can, and do, turn everyday situations into legacy moments. Ironically, you may be the only person who is aware that it is a legacy moment. This is an internal journey of you showing up as your best self and creating special moments. Unless you tell someone that you made a choice to create a legacy moment, they may not notice.

Let me share some examples:

My stressed-out daughter snaps a smart response to my question. Rather than snap back, I respond in love.

My granddaughter wants me to take her to the park after school. Despite a looming book deadline, we spend several hours at the park. She is the queen, and I am her guard.

The grandkids are fighting over a toy. This is my opportunity to talk about values.

My daughter, her husband, and two children are living with us while their house is being built. This co-habitation arrangement has provided unlimited opportunities for me to create legacy moments. From doing my granddaughter's hair in the mornings to tucking my grandchildren in at night.

Legacy moments can be as simple as making the bed so that your bedroom is a peaceful haven. Or it can be as complicated as launching a new industry to help families from suffering the pain of a failed inheritance. Only you can decide if you are creating legacy moments.

Over the years, I've discovered some helpful tools for creating legacy moments. I've included the most impactful tools that have helped me, so you can use them to live your legacy. As you read them, place a checkmark next to the ones that resonate with you.

_____ Live with the end in mind. I often ask myself, "Will this matter in five years?" If it doesn't, I let it go. If it does matter, I do my best

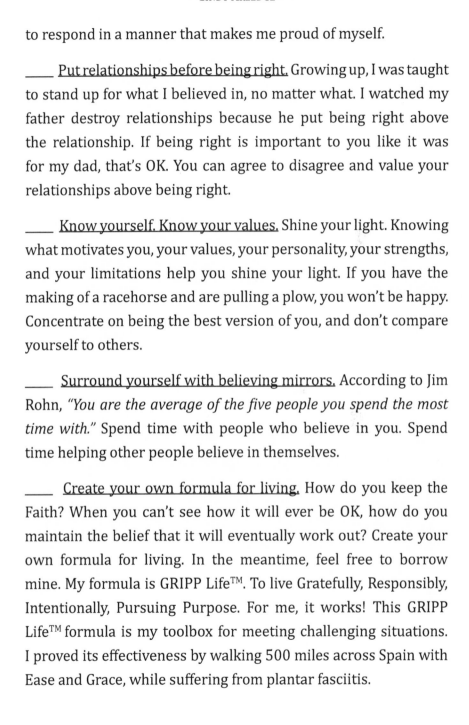

to respond in a manner that makes me proud of myself.

_____ Put relationships before being right. Growing up, I was taught to stand up for what I believed in, no matter what. I watched my father destroy relationships because he put being right above the relationship. If being right is important to you like it was for my dad, that's OK. You can agree to disagree and value your relationships above being right.

_____ Know yourself. Know your values. Shine your light. Knowing what motivates you, your values, your personality, your strengths, and your limitations help you shine your light. If you have the making of a racehorse and are pulling a plow, you won't be happy. Concentrate on being the best version of you, and don't compare yourself to others.

_____ Surround yourself with believing mirrors. According to Jim Rohn, *"You are the average of the five people you spend the most time with."* Spend time with people who believe in you. Spend time helping other people believe in themselves.

_____ Create your own formula for living. How do you keep the Faith? When you can't see how it will ever be OK, how do you maintain the belief that it will eventually work out? Create your own formula for living. In the meantime, feel free to borrow mine. My formula is GRIPP Life™. To live Gratefully, Responsibly, Intentionally, Pursuing Purpose. For me, it works! This GRIPP Life™ formula is my toolbox for meeting challenging situations. I proved its effectiveness by walking 500 miles across Spain with Ease and Grace, while suffering from plantar fasciitis.

_____ <u>Accept what happens.</u> This one is hard sometimes. My brother Richard is serving 16 years in a federal prison for conspiracy to laundry money. From the beginning, he has maintained his innocence.

I don't know why he is where he is, but I don't waste any energy wondering why this has happened. My GRIPP Life™ formula helps me maintain my Faith that everything will work out, even when I can't see it in the moment.

_____ <u>Everyone is doing their best.</u> Brene' Brown's book, *Rising Strong*, showed me that everyone is doing the best they can. Observe yourself and others while embracing this belief. We are all doing the best we can in the moment. When my grandchildren are acting out, I know they are stressed. My job is to find out what they need to do better. Typically, it is a snack or a nap! By the way, the same is true with adults. If you have trouble believing that people are doing the best they can, it is indicative that you don't believe you are doing your best. If this is you, please pick up a copy of Brene' Brown's book. This is an important tool in your toolbox for living your legacy.

_____ <u>Cue up the clown music.</u> We recently remodeled a twenty-year-old house. Like any construction project, it was two steps forward, one step back.

There was one week that felt like ten steps backwards. On Tuesday, I watched the construction crew pour our new concrete porch. On Wednesday, they dug it out, looking for the sprinkler heads they had covered up. On Thursday, I returned the moving van in the rain and discovered my car was blocked in the customer parking lot by trucks returned by other customers. On Friday, the painters over sprayed the walls while painting the kitchen cabinets.

Rather than get mad, I started to see each challenge as a clown jumping out of the clown car at the circus. I could hear the music. And it helped. The problems I faced were irritants. No one's life was at stake. Seeing challenges as clowns allows me to show up as my best self. Rather than get mad, I hear *doot-doot-da-doot-doot, doot-da-da doot*, and laugh. Another clown has joined the party.

_____ Hit your knees. When all else fails, I hit my knees and ask God, "What do you want me to learn? What do you want me to do?"

In summary, Step One: *Live your legacy* is an internal journey for you to create legacy moments. Legacy moments are any situation where you respond as your best self and intentional special moments you create. You responded in alignment with the legacy you have defined.

You now have several tools at your disposal to begin your legacy lifestyle of living with the end in mind.

Step Two:
Prepare Yourself

With your internal compass firmly in place, it's time to prepare your outer world.

In this chapter you will hear the harrowing story of a medical emergency that inspired me to create the Legacy Timeline. I've changed the names and details to protect their identities, but the details are very real.

Then, I will share the four stages of the Legacy Timeline so you can begin creating your contingency plans and prepare yourself.

Finally, we will explore the magic of tidying up your life. Ideas to take care of your stuff now, so that what you leave behind isn't a burden for your family.

Preparing yourself is a lifelong process that gets more exciting every day.

A Pound of Cure

When I received the call from Dan's oldest son, I was shocked to learn he was holding on to life by a thread. Days before, he had been a healthy robust 50-year-old, eager to start a new career.

What started out as a simple surgery to repair his colon turned into one medical emergency after another. The abruptness of his decline surprised everyone.

His three sons contacted Dan's attorney and obtained his medical power of attorney. Each medical emergency precipitated another agonizing life or death decision for their dad. The brothers had to guess what their dad wanted because they had never had a conversation about his wishes.

Dan was physically, emotionally, and mentally incapacitated for months. Between his surgery, medically-induced coma, and tracheotomy, he suffered hospital-induced delirium. He just couldn't make sense of what had happened to him.

He suffered PTSD and tried to escape the hospital. In his weakened condition he fell. More than once. To protect him from hurting himself, he was tied to the bed. The nights were especially hard for Dan.

Unfortunately, his story gets more complicated. Dan had a live-in girlfriend, Angela. Some might say, she was his common-law wife. She claimed to have financial power of attorney but never produced a copy for the boys, or Dan's bank.

The relationship between Angela and Dan's sons was already precarious from previous clashes. She was living in Dan's house and they weren't sure if Dan would recover or not. They didn't push the issue to see if she really had a financial power of attorney, because they didn't want to make matters worse.

The brothers all worked full-time jobs and did the best they could to take turns at night to sit with Dan. They also arranged for family friends, like me, to take shifts. Although Angela didn't work outside the home, she spent little time at the hospital.

She did, however, question the medical decisions made by Dan's sons. As time wore on, tension between them and Angela got worse.

Sadly, the entire time Dan was incapacitated, his bills went unpaid. Dan embraced technology to pay all his bills. But, he failed to tell anyone where he kept his passwords. Angela said she couldn't find them.

On top of this devastating medical emergency, Dan's excellent credit was ruined. His relationship with his boys was severely injured, and his lack of preparation caused unnecessary drama for the people he loved the most.

I'm happy to report that although Dan has additional medical issues to resolve, he returned home and started his new career. Angela is still there. It has taken time, but his sons have started to come around again.

Life can change in a heartbeat. Dan was unprepared for his

unexpected medical emergency. Because he wasn't prepared, an extremely difficult situation was made worse.

Dan and his family's suffering profoundly affected me. Their situation helped me identify the four stages of the legacy timeline, and how to prepare for each stage.

How about you? Are you ready for an emergency? It doesn't have to be medical. Your emergency could be responding to someone else's emergency, or something fun like a month-long trip. What would be the consequences, if today, you walked out the door and disappeared from your everyday life?

Have you prepared your family for the roles they will assume on your behalf? Are they a team who can work together? Do they know where to find your passwords and medical information? Have you chosen your medical power of attorney and financial power of attorney?

What about the reverse? Are you listed as a medical or financial power of attorney for someone else? Do you feel empowered to act for them? Do you have the information you need to fulfill their wishes, or will you have to guess?

Remember Ben Franklin's quote? "An ounce of prevention is worth a pound of cure." The following timeline will help you provide the ounce of prevention you need to create a contingency plan for the last three stages of your Legacy Timeline.

When I worked for Countrywide Home Loans, I helped create a series of contingency plans to roll out a nationwide training program. We preplanned a theoretical playbook for "what ifs" for a multitude of situations that we hoped would never happen.

By the end of the training rollout, we only used two of them, and hadn't thought of everything. But the Contingency Plans helped us roll out a successful nationwide training program with the least amount of stress.

The Legacy Timeline

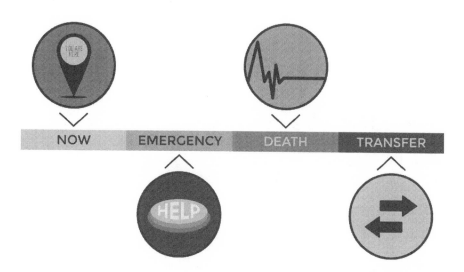

There are four stages on the Legacy Timeline. The stages include:

1. NOW

2. EMERGENCY

3. DEATH

4. TRANSFER

NOW is continuous. Each second is a new NOW, and you may or may not be in an EMERGENCY.

EMERGENCY is a time in your life that you need help. It doesn't have to be a medical emergency. It includes the birth of a child, extended travel, a prison sentence, or just assistance with the aging process. It could be anything that creates the need for assistance from others. Assistance can be physical, financial, emotional, or spiritual.

Asking for help is not easy. In our culture, asking for help is interpreted as weakness. Most people would rather give help than receive help. We are afraid to ask for help, and haven't been trained how to ask for help. We don't understand that the EMERGENCY stage is a natural stage in life.

Learning how to ask for help, especially before we need it, is empowering. At some point in our lives, everyone will need help.

Recognizing the EMERGENCY stage of the Legacy Timeline, and making contingency plans, makes asking for help much easier. It is one of the most powerful tools you can use to reduce stress for you and your loved ones.

DEATH and TRANSFER are one-time events. While the Legacy Family Planning process helps with all stages of life, it is especially important during the DEATH and TRANSFER stages of the Legacy Timeline.

These are very difficult stages for your heirs to get through. Relying on legal, tax, and/or wealth plans to help your family cope isn't fair to them. These plans simply can't equip your heirs for these very emotional stages.

Use the Legacy Timeline to prepare yourself and your heirs for these last stages. Doing so will drastically reduce the drama and stress on your family's relationships during the wealth transfer process.

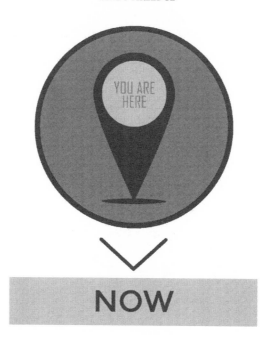

My assumption about you, dear reader, is that you are currently NOT in an EMERGENCY stage. This is the ideal stage to become an Anticipator and create contingency plans to prepare you and your heirs for the final stages of your life.

My assumption is that you can read this from the most enjoyable space you can live: Stephen Covey's quadrant two of **important** but **not urgent**.

If you are familiar with his four quadrants of time management, you are already familiar with the idea of quadrant two activities. If you are not familiar, please add Stephen Covey's book, The *7 Habits of Highly Effective People*, to your reading list.

Quadrant two is acting on **important** but **not urgent** activities. It is the ideal place to live and the ideal place to create plans for the last three stages of your Legacy Timeline.

If my assumption is wrong and your NOW is in the EMERGENCY stage, I'm sorry for you. The drama has already begun. You are in the least desirable energetic place to be: Stephen Covey's quadrant four of **important** and **urgent**. You are already in the chaos of EMERGENCY.

If this describes you, please don't despair. It may be a bit more difficult, but you can still make plans. And, the good news is, this information will help tame the chaos and guide you through the process. It won't be as difficult as it could be.

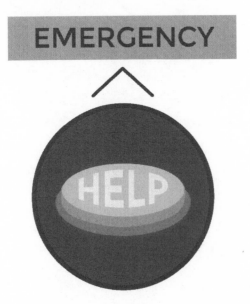

EMERGENCY is the second stage on the Legacy Timeline. In this stage you need help of some kind. This is where contingency planning will reduce the drama for you and your family. Put plans in place before they happen so that your family isn't scrambling to find your passwords to pay your bills. Have conversations with your loved ones. That means two-way conversations. Tell them your desires and ask them if they are willing to help you. Prepare for this stage before it happens.

And if your NOW is also EMERGENCY, it may feel like it is too late to make contingency plans. And, for some, it may be too late. It's important to focus on what CAN be done and don't waste a precious minute on should haves or could haves. I often counsel people and say, "Don't should on yourself."

NOW is the time to ask for help, communicate clearly, and focus on desired outcomes. It's been over twenty years since my nephew survived brain cancer. At the tender age of eleven he endured emergency brain surgery and a year of chemotherapy treatments. The philosophy his father lived by, and one you can use too, is "prepare for the worst and hope for the best."

Your NOW will go in and out of the EMERGENCY stage many times in life.

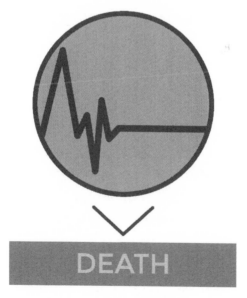

DEATH

DEATH is the third stage on the Legacy Timeline. Your estate plan provides your heirs with the legal means to get through the next two stages of your life, but it isn't designed to help them with their emotions. Do more than provide them with the minimum. Have the courage to talk to them about your end-of-life decisions. Don't make them guess after you've passed away.

Create "case studies" from examples of other people who are dealing with emergencies and deaths around you. For instance, I've already discussed "what if" scenarios with my family in case I am diagnosed with Alzheimer's disease. These are not one and done conversations, but ongoing, as needs and preparations change.

Talking about death and money from a quadrant two perspective makes it easier. *Your heirs may be quite uncomfortable talking about this with you.* Don't give up. Give them a copy of this book. Have conversations that are uncomfortable. Tell them what you want to prevent drama before it happens. Assure them that you are simply preparing for the future and getting your affairs in order. In the end, they will thank you.

Legacy Family Planning is the vehicle to prepare them for this difficult time in life. Do them the favor of facing your mortality, and changing the cultural taboo of addressing these topics in a straight forward manner. More importantly, once you complete the three simple steps in this book, empower them with a Legacy Family Plan by adding the missing link to your estate plan to reduce any unnecessary drama.

TRANSFER

TRANSFER is the final stage on the Legacy Timeline. This may be the most important stage on your timeline. It continues long past your life. Depending on how well you prepare yourself and your family, it could last for generations to come. Imagine your grandchildren's grandchildren benefiting from the gifts you leave behind.

The TRANSFER stage is also one of the most difficult stages to prepare for. You won't be around to affect the outcome or see the results. It is the stage in which your legal, tax, and wealth plans come together to benefit your heirs.

Legacy Family Planning has the potential to transform your TRANSFER stage. When you add this plan to your estate planning process, you can rest easy, confident you have done all you can do to prepare your heirs to receive your legacy.

Use your Legacy Timeline to make plans for all four stages of your life. Once you have completed your contingency planning for the EMERGENCY, DEATH, and TRANSFER stages, your NOW is filled with a string of legacy moments. The sense of peace that comes from being prepared is life-changing.

In Sweden, it is common practice for aging citizens to declutter their home before they die to relieve the burden on their families. This end-of-life practice is called *döstädning* and translates to "death cleaning."

While I love the practicality of the Swedish culture, death cleaning doesn't hold much appeal. I much prefer the Japanese's view of tidying up our life, which is covered in the next section.

Life-Changing Magic

While the Legacy Timeline is a great tool to help you prepare for the four stages of life, there is another aspect of your legacy to consider. Let's talk about your "stuff."

Marie Kondo's *New York Times* bestselling book, *The Life-Changing Magic of Tidying Up: The Japanese Art of Decluttering and Organizing*, provides an interesting method for cleaning out your home.

I enjoyed her book and used some of her ideas to clean out my closets and drawers. But what I love the most about her book, is her title: *The Life-Changing Magic of Tidying Up!*

Yes! There is magic in tidying up your life. There's even more magic when tidying up is part of your Legacy Family Plan.

How do you want to be remembered? What do you want to experience? What do you want to leave behind? These are the three aspects of legacy.

When the purpose behind cleaning up is to ensure the three aspects of your legacy are realized, tidying up takes on a whole new meaning.

This is a lifelong process that gets easier over time. You will want to begin with the most important tasks first. Those tasks that prepare you for the last three stages on your Legacy Timeline.

Begin by organizing your legal documents, important papers, and items your family will need to help you during the EMERGENCY stage in life.

As you read the following list of areas to tidy up, place a checkmark next to the ones that need attention.

Make a list of areas to tidy up, set a date to get them done, and get going. Below are some categories to get you started.

_____ Get a will. In case you haven't gotten your will yet, do it now. Put it in your legacy drawer.

_____ Create a legacy drawer. Dave Ramsey, famous for his Financial Peace University, recommends creating a legacy drawer. A single location of information your family will need to settle your estate. Make it easy for them. Tell your children where to find the documents. Our legacy drawer is a fireproof, locked filing cabinet. Our kids know where to find the key and are familiar with the content.

_____ Write your draft obituary. Write a draft obituary; you'll be glad you did. Write it as a work of fiction. Put all your dreams and goals into it "as if" they were done. It will help you discover what you would still like to experience and how you want to be remembered. Oh, and make sure you put real information in it too, like your parents' legal names. Your children may only remember them as Maw Maw and Paw Paw.

_____ Pictures. I have boxes of pictures I inherited from my parents. The old smelly ones of people I don't know because they aren't labeled, as well as pictures of my brothers and I growing up. I have my parents' vacation pictures, as well as my own. And how about that box of negatives you've been holding onto? How about those digital files? Are they organized?

Pictures bring back memories and remind us of good times. They are difficult to throw away on a good day, impossible in the grip of grief. Do yourself and your children a favor by cleaning out your photo file together. Give them pictures now. If your kids or other relatives don't want them, then toss them.

_____ Personal effects and other stuff. My husband, Gerald, inherited a collection of New Mexico Kachina dolls and sand paintings from his mother. In our journey of life-changing magic, we have decided to let these collections go. Our girls don't want them.

Together, the collections are impressive expressions of Native American art created in the early 1950s. Rather than see them split up and sold in an estate sale, Gerald and I are researching museums that will display them so that others can enjoy their beauty.

_____ Family heirlooms. The older I get, the more important these items become. I know the story behind the glass bowl sitting on the counter top, but my children don't know its significance.

We recently moved to North Texas to be closer to our grandchildren. Now that we spend more time together, I make it a point to share the stories behind our heirlooms with them. It's on my list to put together a book with photos so that the stories are preserved.

_____ Stories. As I've aged, I've become more and more like my mother. She did her best to get me interested in our genealogy. As a single mom, I didn't have time. Now, of course, I regret the lost opportunity.

Realizing what I missed, I now enjoy spending my spare time researching our family history. The Internet has made my search easy compared to what my mother went through to find information.

She always wanted me to become a Daughter of the American Revolution (DAR), but couldn't find the supporting documents. Last year, thanks to technology and tenacity, my girls and I became DAR members, and I can feel Mom's smile from heaven.

Not surprisingly, my girls are equally uninterested at this stage of their lives. Which is why I plan to gather the stories into a book that can be passed down from one generation to the next.

_____ Secrets. Secrets can be dangerous. Will you take a secret to the grave, or will your family find out after you are gone? Is there something your family should know, but you've been afraid to face? One of my clients adopted their granddaughter after she was neglected by their daughter. The granddaughter knows she is adopted, she just doesn't know that her adopted parents are her real grandparents and that her sister is her mother. Taking the risk to share your secrets while you are alive isn't easy. It takes courage to give your family the opportunity to ask you questions.

_____ Jewelry and art. Jewelry and art are very personal purchases. If you have pieces you own, but don't wear or enjoy, ask your children if they want them. If they say yes, go ahead and give those pieces to them now.

If they don't want them, turn them into cash, donate them, or give them to friends who would enjoy them. Clean out your closets, drawers, and storage; let go of anything that you don't love, love, love.

_____ <u>Excess financial assets.</u> How much is enough? If you have assets that you won't ever need for bills, use them to improve the world. Do you have a favorite charity you want to support? Perhaps you can use your excess financial assets to invest in your family's human capital development. How about a family trip? Would setting up an account for your grandchildren's grandchildren education excite you?

Meet with your financial wealth advisor. Share your goals and ask for help. They have the experience and expertise to help you put a plan together to achieve your goals.

In summary, Step Two: *Prepare yourself* by creating contingency plans for the final stages of your life and enjoying the life-changing magic of tidying up. Review the list of items that need attention, and tackle them one step at a time. Use the positive energy of quadrant two, **important** and **not urgent**, to complete step two of your legacy plan.

Step Three: Prepare Your Heirs

With your internal compass firmly in place, and preparations for yourself underway, it's time to prepare your heirs. In doing so, you may well find they help you in ways you couldn't anticipate.

In this chapter you will discover how to bust the family business myth and see your business in a new way.

While the tools from Steps One and Two have helped you live your best life, they also have positively impacted your heirs. In this final chapter, you will receive one more set of tools to help you prepare your family.

Through My Daughter's Eyes

When my parents passed away, I inherited commercial real estate in Texas and Tennessee. Some properties I owned outright, others were co-owned with various partners.

There was a car lot in Memphis co-owned with a brother who refuses to acknowledge my existence. It's been a dozen years since my parents passed away, and he still doesn't speak to me.

Another car lot in south Texas was co-owned by Dad's business partner's children. That's a head scratcher, huh! My father and his business partner have both passed away. My company owns Dad's half, and Dad's business partner's two children inherited the other half.

Additional properties were co-owned with my children, a niece, and nephew.

These properties were added to my own portfolio of real estate that I've owned for twenty years.

My parents' estate plan was complicated, and my inheritance complicated my life. Now, I file over a dozen tax returns each year.

Over time, managing the numerous entities, properties, and partnerships has become second nature. I don't question the complexity of what I do. I just do what needs to be done.

When we started our Legacy Family Plan and hired my daughter, Tiffany, to learn the business, I saw my business through her eyes. In doing so, I saw problems within our portfolio that I had overlooked for years. I saw the myth of the family business.

Through my daughter's eyes, I saw the property that was in an unsafe area. Through her eyes, I saw the difficulty of managing an out-of-state property. And the potential problems created by our partnerships.

With these new insights, I realized that I was setting her up for a disaster. I couldn't pretend everything was OK. It was time to tidy up our portfolio of properties.

The key to success is to make the "next right" decision with the information you have available at the time. Don't second guess your decisions.

It's been four years since I started seeing my business through my daughter's eyes. Although I have thirty years' experience of managing commercial real estate, it has surprised me how long it has taken to tidy up our portfolio.

Step by step, decision by decision, we cleared out our problem properties and wrapped up partnerships.

Seeing my business through my daughter's eyes gave me fresh eyes. She helped me recognize problems that I had become accustomed to handling. I didn't even recognize them as challenges anymore.

I shudder to think what it would have been like for my family if I hadn't seen my business through her eyes. But once I did, I didn't want to leave behind a mess of problems. I know what it is like to inherit a mess, and I don't want my girls to have to deal with problems after I'm gone, if I can prevent them now.

She helped me recognize the family business myth. Through her eyes, I could see the sacrifices my children would have to make to keep the business going. We are currently in the process of making changes in our business plan. We still have work to do, but I am filled with deep appreciation and satisfaction for the tremendous progress we've made in the past few years.

Tools to Prepare Your Heirs

As you read this last set of tools, please keep in mind that you don't have to do this alone. Ask for help if you need it from a trained Legacy Family Planner or other professional advisors. Place a checkmark next to tools that resonate.

_____ <u>Eliminate the environment that the Cur$e thrives in.</u> Help your children heal issues of jealousy, fear, and selfishness. Replace an attitude of entitlement with gratitude. Prepare them to receive their inheritance. Help them move past childhood labels so they can see each other as human beings.

Are there environmental issues to eliminate?

_____ <u>Have fun together.</u> Provide opportunities for your family to spend time and have fun together. Holidays don't count; they are full of stress. We claimed a reoccurring week during the summer to vacation together as a family and travel to different locations. One year it's to Disney World or one of our favorite cities, the next year it's the beach!

What fun activities can you do with your family?

_____ <u>Invest in their success.</u> Over the years we have scheduled workshops and hired professionals from various fields to provide educational sessions for our adult children. After my parents passed away, we brought in an attorney, CPA, financial advisor, and motivational speaker to help our adult children understand the inheritance they received from my parents. Since then, we continue to bring in industry professionals to provide training to improve their knowledge and skills.

What investment can you make for your family's success?

_____ Create your Legacy Impact Statement. Earlier in this book, you answered questions at the end of each capital account. The answers you provided are the framework for your Legacy Impact Statement. Transfer your answers to the blanks below. As a reminder, the three answers include (1) yourself, (2) your current heirs, or (3) unborn generations.

Legacy Impact Statement

I want my Financial Capital to impact _____.

I want my Intellectual Capital to impact _____.

I want my Social Capital to impact _____.

I want my Human Capital to impact _____.

I want my Spiritual Capital to impact _____.

How will you share your Legacy Impact Statement with your family?

_____ Tell a new story. Is your family dysfunctional? If you answered yes, you are not alone. The good news is, your family can change. You can let go of old stories and replace them with a new one. Legacy Family Planning is the missing link that provides the focus and direction to become the family you want to be.

Write your family's new story, and make it a good one!

_____ <u>Create a Family Board of Directors.</u> Do you have the right professional advisors helping you? Will they work together as a team? Will they meet with each other and your entire family on a regular basis?

With the right team, you can create a Family Board of Directors. By meeting regularly, your Board of Directors and family will be set up for success during the TRANSFER stage after you are deceased.

Who will be on your Board of Directors? Set up time to interview them and set up a meeting with your family.

_____ <u>Provide on-the-job training.</u> It doesn't matter if you have a business entity or not, you can provide on-the-job training for your family. Ask them to meet with your professional advisors on *a regular basis*. Depending on your needs, a regular basis may mean once every five years, or once a month. You want your heirs and your professional advisors to be able to communicate with each other. This will prepare them to work together when you are no longer around.

If you own a family business, have the courage to see it through your heirs' eyes. Do you see the family business myth?

Common Mistakes
to Avoid

We all know our fate: no one is getting out of here alive. Excluding suicide, the questions that concern us are *When?* and *How?*

Facing these unknowns can be paralyzing. But avoidance is not an effective plan, and failing to create an estate plan is risky business.

Have you experienced this paralysis? Is there something you've been putting off? Something you know you *should* do, but haven't done yet? How can you move past this issue of procrastination? What can you do to motivate yourself to act?

You have enough information to understand the importance of being prepared. But, you may still fail to act. In this chapter I will share the most common mistakes I've seen. Recognizing them for what they are, mistakes, will help you get unstuck. Be willing to be vulnerable, have meaningful conversations, and be fearless in facing your own mortality.

I recognize that polite conversationalists don't speak of such things. Death and money remain taboo topics. But I am not polite. More than once, I have deflated the energy in a room by answering the question, "What do you do?"

When you have the same conversation repeatedly, you begin to see patterns emerge. These patterns reveal common mistakes that prevent people from creating their estate plan. While most generally recognize the need to create a plan, they will quote one of six common mistakes to explain *why a plan isn't right for them right now.*

They don't see the wisdom of Ben Franklin's advice:

> *"An ounce of prevention
> is worth a pound of cure."*

As you read them, see which ones resonate. Place a checkmark next to all that apply.

____   **This isn't a priority right now.**

"You don't understand, Cindy. I've got too much to do. The sink is full of dishes, the laundry is piled up, the dog is sick, and this isn't a priority right now."

Overwhelm. I get it. If this describes you, you are not alone. When I begin working with clients who have overcome this mistake, they tell me they are just trying to get through the day. Their focus is one day at a time.

When you expand your focus to living with the end in mind, your life gets easier. Instead of feeling overwhelmed because you are trying to get through the day, this broader perspective allows you to focus on what's important, and laugh at what isn't important.

____   **I have time to do it later.**

"Cindy, I'll take care of this later. As soon as I finish (fill in the blank) I will contact my attorney. It's on my list to do."

The road to hell is paved with good intentions. We think we have time, until it's too late. Everyone knows someone who died unexpectedly and left their family unprotected. Don't let this be you.

Relief, peace of mind, and confidence. These are the bi-products of getting your estate plan in place. Once you check it off the "to do" list, you feel energized and eager to do more.

_____ **That won't happen to us.**

"Cindy, you don't understand. Our family isn't like that. We are close and never fight. We have a will in place and don't need to do anything else."

One of my favorite quotes dates to 1741. Paraphrasing a German Theologian, Johann Kaspar Lavater:

> *"You don't really know someone*
> *until you share an inheritance with them."*

I've seen a family destroyed over $11 per month gas royalty checks. Martin Luther King Jr.'s family fought 48 years over a bible and his Nobel Peace Prize Medal. Receiving personal effects and financial assets from our loved ones is an emotional process. You cannot predict how your family will respond after you are gone.

While you can't predict how they will respond, you can prepare your heirs. I'll never forget one of my dad's best friends asking me to lunch after Dad died. He tried to convince me that Dad said he could have his diamond belt buckle. This family friend was just one of many who tried to hustle me after Dad was gone.

Have conversations about personal items while you are alive. If you are willing to let it go, give it to them while you are alive to watch them enjoy your gift.

My friend's mom courageously battled cancer for years. She was married to a second husband, and there were problems. While she was alive, she quietly gave away all her jewelry. Upon her death, he discovered the loss and pulled out a gun and threatened to shoot my friend. How incredibly wise it was to make these early gifts.

_____ **It's not my problem. I'll be gone.**

"Cindy, I'll be gone, what do I care? It's not my problem."

Ouch. Most people who say this, don't mean it. But, some do. This statement is a direct response to feeling helpless or overwhelmed about how to go about transferring their wealth. Many have experienced a failed inheritance and are familiar with the challenges their family members face. They are frustrated because they don't know what to do, so they say they don't care.

When I share the missing link for transferring wealth without drama, the people who really don't care, don't care. The ones who do care, but don't have the information to help their family, are excited about the process of CRACKING the Inheritance Code.

_____ **Our problems are too big. This won't work.**

"Cindy, I wish you could help. We don't get along now, and I don't have the energy to try."

There are some families that are too broken to mend. Not every family will become a Legacy Family. But throwing in the towel without trying is a disservice to you, and your family.

While you are still alive to answer questions and communicate with your heirs, your Legacy Family Planning advisor can facilitate conversations, manage expectations, and address any conflicts. If there is a permanent split in the family, helping your family members cope with this loss while you are alive will help them after you are gone.

_____ I can't afford this.

"Cindy, I would if I could, but I can't afford this."

Tight budget. I get it. If this describes you, you are not alone. When I work with clients who have overcome this mistake, they tell me that the sacrifice they made to ensure their family's future was one of the best investments they ever made. They slept better at night knowing their family was safe.

Like any goal you set, once you commit to achieving it, you are relentless in your quest. Many clients get creative in funding their wills. One client traded his editing services with his attorney. Another received his will as a Christmas gift. Once you see the value, making the investment is easy.

Did any of the common mistakes resonate with you? Are you willing to get slightly uncomfortable to protect your family? Avoid letting these common mistakes force you into quadrant four time management of **important** and **urgent** or prevent you from creating your ounce of prevention. Avoid these common mistakes so you can avoid the issues and drama that Dan and his family experienced.

Before We End, Let's Review

This book was divided into three parts. In Part One, we reviewed some things you know and some things you may be trying to avoid. These included:

- No one is getting out of here alive.

- Everyone over the age of 18 needs a will.

- Money is an Amplifier.

- The Cur$e of Inheritance is real.

- The Three Generational Cycle of Wealth is a world-wide issue.

- Unresolved differences of perspective cause unnecessary drama.

- Introduction to the Legacy Pyramid Assessment.

Through this book you have probably discovered many things you didn't know. Part Two was dedicated to helping you learn what you didn't know that you didn't know.

- The three aspects to legacy include your memories, experiences, and possessions. Each morning and evening, review the answers to the three important questions.

- The five capital accounts include financial, intellectual, social, human, and spiritual.

- We discovered the secret of successful wealth transfer.

- Legacy Family Planning is the missing link for successfully transferring wealth and cracking the inheritance code.

- You completed the Legacy Pyramid Assessment.

- Discovered what you and your family can expect at the Avoider, Acceptor, and Anticipator levels of the Legacy Pyramid.

- You debunked the family business myth that the family business is the best vehicle for transferring wealth to subsequent generations.

In Part Three, you learned the three simple steps for CRACKING the Inheritance Code and transferring wealth without drama.

- Live your legacy.

- Prepare yourself.

- Prepare your family.

Embrace Irony

At the beginning of this book, I asked you to be alert to irony and shared some of the life lessons I've learned by embracing irony.

Rejection taught me to accept myself. Hate taught me to love. Death taught me how to live my best life. Most importantly, irony helped me turn the biggest mess of my life into a message to help you. Now, it's your turn.

I invite you to expand your vision, to live with the end in mind so you can enjoy the preciousness of the moment. Bring context to challenges. Ask yourself the following questions: Will this be important in a week? A month? A year? Five years?

I invite you to embrace irony. See challenges as opportunities to be your best self. To respond to challenges in alignment with how you want to be remembered.

I invite you to experience life, fulfill your dreams. An important aspect of your legacy is enjoying experiences that have been placed in your heart. Create shared memories and experiences with your family. Have fun together.

I invite you to enjoy the magic of tidying up your life. Enjoy the freedom of less is more. An important aspect of your legacy is what you leave behind. Make sure you see your legacy through your children's eyes so that the capital you leave behind is a blessing and not a burden.

And remember, your legacy is much richer than financial assets. In addition to your financial capital, you have intellectual, social, human, and spiritual capital accounts to share.

Transform fear of dying into inspiration to live your best life. Discover the peace and confidence that comes from facing death. Although it is a lifelong process, after you have your contingency plan in place you can enjoy the feeling of peace that you are prepared for emergencies and a smooth transfer of wealth at the end of your life. Avoid the problems, drama, and heartbreaks that happen to unprepared heirs and loved ones. Prepare for the worst and hope for the best.

Use the tools I've shared to complete the simple, but not easy, steps to define your legacy. Prepare yourself and prepare your heirs. Doing so will become your roadmap for living your dream life and leaving your legacy. Prepare your family to thrive in your absence.

CRACKING the Inheritance Code for transferring wealth without drama is the surprising gift you give yourself. It is the roadmap for making each day a gift. Enjoy living your legacy every day.

To jumpstart your journey, I have included a contract for you to sign with yourself. Signing this contract signals your commitment to the process and an easy success to build momentum. Sign the contract to make the commitment and celebrate completing this important first step.

You can sign below in the print book, or download a copy at

www.legacyfamilyrevolution.com/commit

CONTRACT

I, _____, understand I am beginning a journey to define my legacy. I commit to the three simple steps to prepare myself and my heirs, so that my legacy is a joy to live and a blessing to give.

I, _____, further understand that this process will have ups and downs. I commit to asking for help, embracing irony, searching for new ideas and tools to add to the ones provided in this book, and being tenacious in my journey of CRACKING the Inheritance Code.

_____

(Signature)

_____

(Date)

An Invitation

Now that you have seen a fresh new approach to an age old problem, learned what you didn't know that you didn't know, implemented the three simple steps to live your legacy, and signed your contract, I invite you to take the next right step.

Keep the momentum going. Pick up your copy of the *Legacy Family Way* to add the missing link to your estate plan. If you would like help with your Legacy Family Plan, we would be honored to help. For more information, visit our website:

www.legacyfamilyrevolution.com

Legacy Family Planning is the best method that successful families use to prevent the Cur$e of Inheritance, beat the three-generational cycle of shirtsleeves to shirtsleeves, and create lasting family wealth.

Remember the poem at the beginning of this book that impacted me? It lays provides the framework for developing personal happiness and passing it on to your children. Together, you just might change the world.

"The most precious inheritance that parents can give their children is their own happiness."

—Thich Nhat Hanh

Ironically, Legacy Family Planning is the process for transferring your satisfaction and happiness to your heirs. Preparing your family for life after you're gone is also the path for creating meaningful memories they will cherish forever. These memories become the story of your family passed to future generations. This is your legacy. This is the inheritance that your family deserves.

About the Author

CINDY ARLEDGE, MBA is a three-time bestselling author, speaker, and visionary leader of the Legacy Family Revolution. Her company is the place where family leaders and estate planning professionals can find useful information, training, and support to transfer wealth without drama.

After surviving the destruction of her own family following her parents' deaths, Cindy vowed to help other families avoid common pitfalls that plague the majority of wealth transfer events. She is passionate about providing affordable Legacy Family Planning to families and business owners.

An active philanthropist, Cindy helped raise over 3 million dollars to build a women's shelter in Boerne, TX.

In 2017, Cindy and her husband, Gerald, left the Texas Hill Country to return to the Dallas area to spend more time with their growing family.

Please join the Revolution Now!

Website: http://www.LegacyFamilyRevolution.com

Facebook: http://www.Facebook.com/LegacyFamilyRevolution

LinkedIn: https://www.LinkedIn.com/in/cindyarledge

Amazon Author Page: http://www.Amazon.com/author/cindyarledge

Website: http://www.LegacyFamilyPlannersAssociation

About the Illustrator

LISA ROTHSTEIN is the award-winning Madison Avenue ad agency copywriter and creative director best known for creating the famous "Wait'll We Get Our Hanes on You" campaign that changed America's underwear.

In her own creative consulting business, she uses a combo of cartooning and cutting-edge marketing strategy and language to help companies and entrepreneurs see their ideal clients and present their products, brand and message in a new and unforgettable way. She has both authored and illustrated Amazon best sellers in the business space. For creative consulting or cartoon projects: www.lisarothstein.com/cartoons

Hire a Certified Legacy Family Planner to Speak at Your Event!

Are you looking for an attention-grabbing keynote speaker who will deliver a fresh new idea with a powerful message that adds to the long-term life success of your people?

Legacy Family Planning is the best kept secret used by elite families who want to transfer values, character, and wealth to future generations without the drama. Staggering to consider that, on average, more than half of your audience doesn't even have a Last Will & Testament.

Contact our office to **book a Certified Legacy Family Speaker as your keynoter** and you're not only securing a profoundly impactful part of your program, you're investing in the long-term success of your people and their family's future.

For more info, visit
www.LegacyFamilyRevolution.com
or call +1 (210) 414-7522 today.

Motivate and
Inspire Others

Share a printed copy of this book.

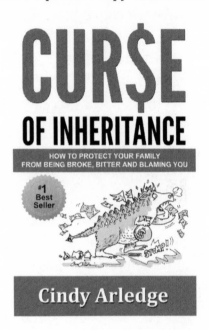

Retail: $20.00
Special Quantity Discounts

5-20 Books	$17.50
21-49 Books	$9.95
50+ Books	$6.50

To place an order, contact:
210-414-7522
www.LegacyFamilyRevolution.com
info@LegacyFamilyRevolution.com

Are you inspired
to help others?

Consider joining the growing number
of professional advisors.

Limited Spaces Available

A Business with Purpose

For more information, contact:
210-414-7522
www.LegacyFamilyPlannersAssociation.com
info@LegacyFamilyPlannersAssociation.com

Notes

Made in the USA
San Bernardino, CA
13 April 2018